Presented to

_____

by

_____

on

_____

Scriptures quoted from the *International Children's Bible®, New Century Version®*, copyright © 1986, 1988, 1999 by Tommy Nelson™, a division of Thomas Nelson, Inc., Nashville, Tennessee 37214. Used by permission.

09 08 07 06 05 04   9 8 7 6 5 4 3

stories retold by Susan L. Lingo

illustrated by Kathy Parks

Standard
Publishing
cincinnati, ohio

Contents

New Testament

Bedtime Rhyme

(to the tune of "Twinkle, Twinkle, Little Star")

Twinkle, twinkle, starry-shine,
(hold hands high and "twinkle" your fingers)

now it's Bible story time.
(hold hands side by side, like an open book)

We can learn of God above,
(point upward)

read of Jesus and his love.
(give yourself a hug)

Let's get ready right away
(move fists in circles in "hurrying" motion)

and be with God to end our day.
(hold hands in prayer position)

Hi, I'm Night-Light,
your special firefly friend!

If you look closely,
you will find me
in one of the pictures
of every story you read.
I love to read
Bible stories.
Let's read them
together!

God Made the World

God said, "I made the earth." Isaiah 45:12

Who made the world?
God made the world!
God made light and God made air.
God made green plants everywhere.
And it was good.
What do you see in the world?

Who made the world?
God made the world!
God made the fish.
God made the sky.
God made animals and people, oh my!
And it was good.
What do you see in the world?

 How many swishy fish do you see?

Who made the world?
God made the world!
God made the world.
God made it the best.
Then what did God make?
God made REST.
And it was very good.
Night-night!

Count the stars.

Quiet Time

Night-Light has some questions.
- Who made the world?
- What did God say?
  "I made the earth."
- How can you thank God for the world?

Prayer Time

Dear God,
Thank you for the wondrous world
you made with so much love.
Thank you for the earth below
and for the stars above.
Amen.

Sleep Time

Tonight's Bible word is **world**.
God's world is so great. What's
your favorite part of the world?
Sleep tight!

God's Promise

God said, "What God promises, he keeps." Numbers 23:19

God was sad; people everywhere disobeyed him.
God would make it rain and wash the world clean.
But God loved Noah and promised to keep him safe.
"Build a boat," said God. And Noah obeyed God.
God sent every kind of animal to ride on the ark.
Then it began to rain and rain.

Drip, drop, pouring down—
rain was falling all around!
God promised to keep Noah, his family,
And the animals safe in the ark—and God did.
God always keeps his promises!
But there was so much water!
Drip, drip, drop—
would the rain ever stop?

 Find a fish and a frog.

Yes! God stopped the rain.
The flood began to go down, down, down—
just as God had promised!

Noah opened the window
and sent a pretty dove to find dry land.
And the bird found a green leaf!
Noah knew there was dry land.
Noah was thankful to God.
God had kept his promise!

Name the rainbow colors.

Quiet Time

Night-Light has some questions.

- Who stopped the rain?
- What did God say?
  "What God promises, he keeps."
- Who always keeps his promises?

Prayer Time

Dear God,
Thank you for your promises—
each one you always keep.
Promise now to keep me safe
tonight while I'm asleep.
Amen.

Sleep Time

Tonight's Bible word is **promise**.
Think about God's promise of love.
Sleep tight!

The Oh-No Tower

God said, "Remember that I am God." Isaiah 46:9

Long ago, people thought they were very smart.
They said, "There's no one smarter than us, not one!
We're smarter than God—or anyone!"
But were they smarter than God?
Oh, no! God is smarter than anyone.

The people wanted to be like God.
So they built a tall, tall, touch-the-sky tower.
Up and up they piled the bricks.
And as they worked, they said,
"There's no one wiser than us, not one!
We're wiser than God—or anyone!"
But were they wiser than God?
Oh, no! God is wiser than anyone.

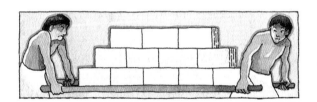

 How many blocks are the men carrying?

The tower was tall.
The people were happy.
But was God happy?
Oh, no!
God came down and scrambled
the people's words around.
The people could not understand each other.
They spread out.
The people went all about!
They learned that no one is wiser than God.
Oh, yes!

Quiet Time

Night-Light has some questions.
- What did the people say?
- What did God say?
    "Remember that I am God."
- Who is wiser than anyone?

Prayer Time

Dear God,
You're the wisest in every way.
We will follow you each day.
Amen.

Sleep Time

Tonight's Bible word is **wise**.
Think about how wise God is and
how he helps us every day.
Sleep tight!

Abraham Trusts God

God said, "They will trust in the Lord." Zephaniah 3:12

Abraham and Sarah lived in a comfy-cozy house.
One day, God told Abraham to move to a new land.
God would lead the way.
Abraham didn't want to move.
But Abraham trusted God.
What do you think Abraham did?

Abraham packed!
Abraham packed this, Sarah packed that—
they took all their clothes and their little white cat.
Then march, march, march—
Abraham and Sarah followed God.
And they trusted God, too.
What a parade it was!

 Point to Abraham. Find the cat.

God led Abraham and Sarah to a new land.
God was happy that Abraham trusted him.
Abraham looked up. What did he see?
Trillions of twinkly stars!
Then God promised Abraham that his family
would be as many as the stars in the sky.
That's a big family!
Thank you, God.

Point to the tent. Who is in the tent?

Quiet Time

Night-Light has some questions.
- Who did Abraham trust?
- What did God say?
  "They will trust in the Lord."
- Who can you trust?

Prayer Time

*Dear God,
We know you love us so.
Please help our trust in you to grow.
Amen.*

Sleep Time

Tonight's Bible word is **trust**.
Think about how nice it feels to
trust God and know he loves us.
Good night!

Baby in a Basket

God said, "I will save you." Jeremiah 30:10

Baby Moses needed a safe place to hide.
But where?
Mother and Miriam, Moses' sister, thought and thought.
Mother got an idea!
She wove a grassy basket bin to put her precious baby in!
What did Mother do then?

Mother put baby Moses in his cozy basket.
Then she set the basket in the tall, cool grass by the river.
Miriam peeked through grass
to make sure baby Moses was safe.
Peekaboo!
We see you, baby Moses!
Oh! Someone's coming!
Who could it be?

Find baby Moses. Point to Miriam.

A princess!
The princess picked up the precious baby.
Miriam asked the princess if she
wanted help with the baby.
Who did Miriam get to help?
Baby Moses' mother!
Mother and Miriam and Moses could
be together again.
"Sleep tight, baby Moses," Mother said.
"I'll cuddle you and stay right here,
and God will keep you safe, my dear!"

Where is the princess?

Quiet Time

Night-Light has some questions.

- Where did Mother hide Moses?
- What did God say?
  "I will save you."
- How do you feel when God keeps you safe?

Prayer Time

Dear God,
Our Father up above,
you keep us safe with all your love.
We don't ever have to fear
because you are always near.
Amen.

Sleep Time

Tonight's Bible word is **safe**.
Think about how good it is to know
that we're safe because God loves us.
Sleep tight!

Red Sea Run

God said, "I will save you." Jeremiah 30:10

Once there was a mean king.
He didn't like God's people.
And he didn't like God.

But God loved his people and would keep them safe.
So God spoke to Moses from a burning bush.
God told Moses to lead his people
away from the mean king.
The mean king was angry and chased them!
Run, Moses, run—lead God's people free!
Run, Moses, run—but what about the sea?

The Red Sea was very big.
The Red Sea was very deep.
Could the sea stop God?
No, sirree!

 Who is wearing a red robe?

God did an amazing thing.
WHOOSH!—God split the sea in half!
Moses and God's people walked
safely to the other side.
Then Moses thanked God for keeping them safe.
Walk, Moses, walk—God set you free.
God can do anything—
yes, sirree!

Where is Moses?

Quiet Time

Night-Light has some questions.
- Who split the Red Sea?
- What did God say?
  "I will save you."
- Who keeps you safe?

Prayer Time

Dear God,
Thank you for your power and
your awesome might.
You keep us safe
both day and night.
Amen.

Sleep Time

Tonight's Bible word is **safe**.
Think about God's love and how
he keeps us safe. Sleep tight!

God's Ten Rules

God said, "Obey me." Jeremiah 7:23

Moses loved and obeyed God.
When God called Moses up the mountain, Moses obeyed.
And when God told Moses to listen, Moses obeyed.

What did God tell Moses?
God gave Moses ten special rules for the people to obey.
God told us he is God and we should worship only him.
God told us to love him and respect his name.
God told us to take a day of rest.
God told us to love our mommies and daddies.
God told us never, never to hurt anyone.
God told us husbands and wives should be true to each other.
God told us not to steal or ever tell a lie.
And God told us to be happy with what we have.
Then God wrote his rules on two stone tablets.
What good rules to obey!

 How many stone tablets do you see?

Why did God give us special rules?
God gave us rules because he loves us.
God gave us rules to keep us safe and happy.
And God gave us his special rules to obey.
When we obey God's rules,
we show that we love God.
Thank you, God!
Thank you for your special rules!

Point to a bird in a nest.

Quiet Time

Night-Light has some questions.
- What did God give us?
- What did God say?
  "Obey me."
- Whose special rules can
  you obey?

Prayer Time

Dear God,
Your rules help us every day.
Help us to trust them and obey.
Amen.

Sleep Time

Tonight's Bible word is **rules**.
Think about rules that keep us safe
and how happy God is
when we obey him.
Good night!

God Helps Joshua

God said, "I will help you." Isaiah 41:10

Joshua was God's brave soldier.
Jericho was a city where the people didn't love God.
So God decided to give Jericho to Joshua and his people.
But oh my! A big, tall, can't-get-over-it wall
was around the city!
How could Joshua get over that wall?
God would help!

God told Joshua, all the soldiers, and all the priests
to march around the wall.
Right foot, left foot—step, step, step!
God told them to march around the wall seven times.
Round and round they all marched. 1, 2, 3, 4, 5, 6, 7!
Then God told them to blow their horns.
Tootle, toot—what a sound!
Tootle, toot—and the walls fell . . .

 How many trumpets do you see?

DOWN!
Tumble tower, tumble down—
till every brick is on the ground!
God brought that tall wall down!
Joshua, all the soldiers, and all the priests
shouted with joy to God.
God had helped them!
And God helps us, too.
Thank you, God!

How many bricks are tumbling down?

Quiet Time

Night-Light has some questions.
- What did God tell Joshua?
- What did God say?
  "I will help you."
- Who always helps us?

Prayer Time

Dear God,
We're glad you're always there
to help us out because you care!
Amen.

Sleep Time

Tonight's Bible word is **help**.
Think about how God helps you
and loves you. Night-night!

Ruth and Naomi Are Friends

God said, "Love your neighbor." Leviticus 19:18

Ruth and Naomi were good friends.
They shared a house. And they shared the work.
Ruth swept the floors while Naomi washed the dishes.
And Naomi shared God with Ruth.
Naomi told Ruth all about God's love.
And soon, Ruth loved God as much as Naomi did.

Then one day, something sad happened.
Ruth and Naomi were left alone.
Their husbands had died.
What should they do?
Where should they go?
Naomi wanted Ruth to go back home
to live with her family.
But would Ruth go?

 Point to two furry friends.

Oh, no!
Ruth loved Naomi and wanted to stay with her.
Ruth knew that God brings us good friends,
and friends stick together.
So Ruth stayed with Naomi.
Ruth and Naomi were friends forever!

Count the dogs. Where is the circle shape?

Quiet Time

Night-Light has some questions.
- Who brings us good friends?
- What did God say?
  "Love your neighbor."
- How can you thank God for
  your friends?

Prayer Time

Dear God,
We thank you for our friends.
Please help us
share and care for them.
Amen.

Sleep Time

Tonight's Bible word is **friends**.
Think about the good friends
God has given you.
Good night, friend!

David and Goliath

God said, "I will make you strong." Isaiah 45:5

David had seven brothers.
David wasn't as big as his brothers.
And David wasn't as strong as his brothers.
David was the littlest brother of all!
But David loved God.
And David knew God was bigger and stronger
than anyone or anything. Yes, sirree!

Goliath was a big, BIG guy—and a meanie.
Goliath didn't love God.
He laughed and said, "No one's bigger
or stronger than me!"
No, no, Goliath!
God is bigger and stronger than everyone!
David wanted to stop Goliath from laughing at God.
But David was so little—what could he do?

 Point to the sheep David cared for.

David asked for God's help.
Then David took a smooth stone from the ground.
He swung his sling round and round,
and—zing! plop!—Goliath fell down!
God helped David topple the mean giant.
Yeah, David! Yeah, God!
Let us clap and let us sing—
God is bigger than anything!

How many stones do you see?

Quiet Time

Night-Light has some questions.

- How did God help David?
- What did God say?
  "I will make you strong."
- Who is bigger and stronger than anything?

Prayer Time

Dear God,
We're glad you're who you are—
so big and full of might!
You keep us safe all day long
and in our sleep at night.
Amen.

Sleep Time

Tonight's Bible word is **strong**.
Think about how strong God is.
Night-night!

Daniel Prays

God said, "I will answer you." Jeremiah 33:3

Daniel loved God very much. He prayed to God day and night.
Daniel worked hard and King Darius was happy.
He wanted to put Daniel in charge of his whole kingdom!
But some other men were jealous.
So they plotted and planned.

The men went to King Darius and said,
"O King Darius, you are so great and true.
People should pray only to you!"
So King Darius wrote a law that said:
"NO PRAYING TO GOD FOR 30 DAYS."
But Daniel loved God and kept praying every day.
Because of the law, King Darius had to punish Daniel.

 Point to Daniel. Point to King Darius.

53

Daniel was tossed in the lions' den with
growly-scowly lions! Daniel was afraid,
but he kept praying to God.
"Dear God, I'll always pray to you
no matter what men say or do!"
As Daniel prayed, the lions growled and scowled
and snarled! But God answered Daniel's prayers.
God sent an angel to close the lions' mouths.
Then King Darius knew God is more powerful than
anything and told all the people to pray to God.

 How many growly lions do you see?

Quiet Time

Night-Light has some questions.
- Who kept praying to God?
- What did God say?
  "I will answer you."
- When can you pray?

Prayer Time

Dear God,
We bow our heads to pray
and say we love you every day.
Amen.

Sleep Time

Tonight's Bible word is **pray**.
Think about how good it is to pray
to God. Night-night.

55

God Answers Jonah

God said, "I will answer you." Jeremiah 33:3

The people of Nineveh didn't obey God.
God told Jonah to tell the people, "Obey me."
But what did Jonah say? "Oh, no! I won't go!"
Jonah did not want to talk to the mean people.
So Jonah ran and hid from God.
No, no, Jonah! You can't hide from God!

Jonah jumped into the sea. Kersplash!
He sank down, down, down, until—glip-glup—
a big fish swallowed him up!
For three days and nights, Jonah sat in the belly of the fish.
It smelled pretty awfulish!
Jonah was sorry he'd disobeyed,
so Jonah just sat there and prayed and prayed.

 What is Jonah doing?

But did God answer Jonah's prayers?
Yes, he did!
God always answers our prayers.
God made the big fish spit Jonah out—
pftuwee!
Jonah was safe!
Jonah was thankful that God answers prayers.
What did Jonah do then?
He obeyed and ran to Nineveh!

Quiet Time

Night-Light has some questions.
- What did Jonah do in the fish?
- What did God say?
  "I will answer you."
- Who will answer your prayers?

Prayer Time

Dear God,
Each time we pray to you,
we know you'll hear
and answer, too.
Amen.

Sleep Time

Tonight's Bible word is **answers**.
Think about how God hears
and answers all your prayers.
Night-night.

Happy Birthday, Jesus!

God said, "I am with you." Jeremiah 30:11

What a quiet night it was!
Mary and Joseph walked along the road.
Mary smiled. She knew God's promise was near.
Mary knew that the baby she would have
was God's greatest promise.
But Mary was tired. So was Joseph—yawwwn!

After a while, they came to the town of Bethlehem.
Joseph asked if there were any rooms.
"No room, no room," said the innkeeper.
Everywhere Joseph looked, it was the same.
No room here, no room there.
But God was watching—he would care.
And he did. God led them to a cozy stable.
Then late that night, just before morn . . .

 What is the innkeeper saying?

God's tiny baby Son was born!
Mary wrapped him in a blanket tight,
and Jesus slept in a manger that night.
In that still quiet night, God sent his Son to us.
God promised the world a Savior and
Prince of Peace.
And God always keeps his promises!
Jesus came to save us.
Jesus came to give us peace.
And Jesus came to love us.
Happy birthday, Jesus! We love you, too.

Quiet Time

Night-Light has some questions.
- Who sent Jesus to us?
- What did God say?
  "I am with you."
- How can you tell Jesus you love him?

Prayer Time

Dear God,
Thank you for sending
your Son from above.
Jesus is our Prince of Peace
and the one we love.
Amen.

Sleep Time

Tonight's Bible word is **Jesus**.
Think about the special night when Jesus was born and how much God loves us. Sleep tight.

Where's Jesus?

Jesus said, "Learn from me." Matthew 11:29

As Jesus grew up, he learned more and more
about God, his Father.
God gave Jesus great wisdom and love.
One day, Mary and Joseph took Jesus to the big city.
They went to Jerusalem for a special festival.
It was a time to honor and thank God for his love.
The city was busy, busy, busy.
When it was time to go home,
Mary and Joseph couldn't find Jesus!
Where was Jesus?

Mary and Joseph were so worried—
back and forth they searched and scurried!
They looked for Jesus in the square.
They searched for Jesus everywhere.
Where was Jesus?

 Point to the kitten.

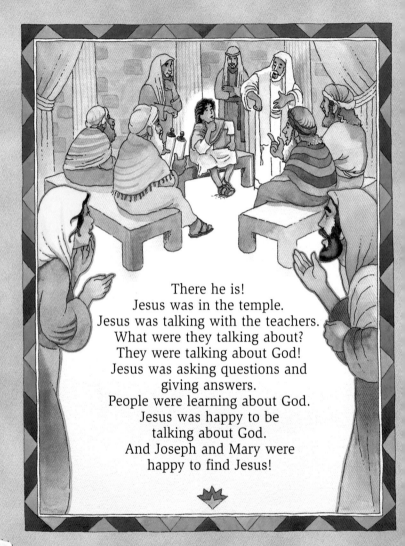

There he is!
Jesus was in the temple.
Jesus was talking with the teachers.
What were they talking about?
They were talking about God!
Jesus was asking questions and
giving answers.
People were learning about God.
Jesus was happy to be
talking about God.
And Joseph and Mary were
happy to find Jesus!

Quiet Time

Night-Light has some questions.
- Where was Jesus?
- What did Jesus say?
  "Learn from me."
- How can you learn about God?

Prayer Time

Dear God,
Please help us learn about you—
about the Bible and Jesus, too.
Amen.

Sleep Time

Tonight's Bible word is **learn**.
Think about how happy God is
when we learn about him.
Night-night.

Follow-Me Fishermen

Jesus said, "Follow me." Matthew 4:19

One day, Jesus was walking beside the Sea of Galilee.
Jesus saw many things.
Jesus saw boats and birds.
Jesus saw waves and water.
And Jesus saw fish and fishermen.

Two of the fishermen were brothers.
Peter and Andrew were catching fish in their nets.
They looked up and saw Jesus walking toward them.
Jesus looked at them and said,
"Come, follow me and I will make you fishers of men."
At once, Peter and Andrew dropped their fishing nets.
They wanted to go with Jesus.
They wanted to follow him and learn about God.
Where did they go?

 How many fish are in the net?

They went to look.
They went to find more
people who wanted
to know, love, and follow Jesus.
We can be like Peter and Andrew.
We can follow Jesus, too!
And we can tell
other people about him!

What are the brothers doing?

Quiet Time

Night-Light has some questions.
- Who were the two brothers?
- What did Jesus say?
  "Follow me."
- How can we know, love, and
  follow Jesus?

Prayer Time

Dear God,
Please help us follow you
in all we say and all we do.
Amen.

Sleep Time

Tonight's Bible word is **follow**.
Think about how we can follow
Jesus and learn about him.
Good night.

Jesus Stops the Storm

Jesus said, "Don't be afraid." Matthew 10:31

One night, Jesus and his friends climbed into a boat.
Stars sparkled. The moon twinkled.
Waves rocked the little boat
back and forth, back and forth.
Yawwwn—Jesus was sleepy.
He lay down and fell fast asleep.
Shhh! Don't wake Jesus.

Then all of a sudden—boom, crash, BOOM!
What a storm!
The rain drummed—ratta-tat-tat!
The wind blew—ooo-ooo-ooo!
Water splashed into the boat.
Jesus' friends were afraid. They woke Jesus.
"What if we sink? What if we drown?
How can you sleep with the rain pouring down?"
What did Jesus do?

 Can you blow like the wind?

Jesus said, "Wind, stop! Waves, stop!"
Did the wind and waves obey him? They did!
The waves stopped flowing.
The wind stopped blowing.
Everyone was safe.
Jesus' friends asked, "Who is this
who can stop a storm?"
Who is this? It's Jesus!
Jesus keeps us safe so we don't have to be afraid.
Thank you, Jesus!

Quiet Time

Night-Light has some questions.
- How did Jesus help his friends?
- What did Jesus say?
    "Don't be afraid."
- Who keeps you safe?

Prayer Time

Dear God,
We're glad for Jesus' love
that you give to all you've made.
We know with Jesus by our side
we'll never be afraid.
Amen.

Sleep Time

Tonight's Bible word is **safe**.
Think about how God keeps you
safe all day and all night.
Night-night!

Dinner for 5,000

Jesus said, "Help other people freely." Matthew 10:8

Look at all the people who were listening to Jesus!
They were learning about God and his love.
But—grumble, grumble—their tummies were hungry!
Where could they eat? Where would they find food?
Jesus' friends were worried.
So many people, so many hungry tummies!
What would Jesus do?

Andrew saw a little boy with a food basket.
What's in the basket?
Tasty bread and yummy fish.
The little boy wanted to share his meal with Jesus.
But how could five loaves of bread and two small fish
fill so many hungry, grumbly tummies?
What would Jesus do?

 Count the loaves and fish.

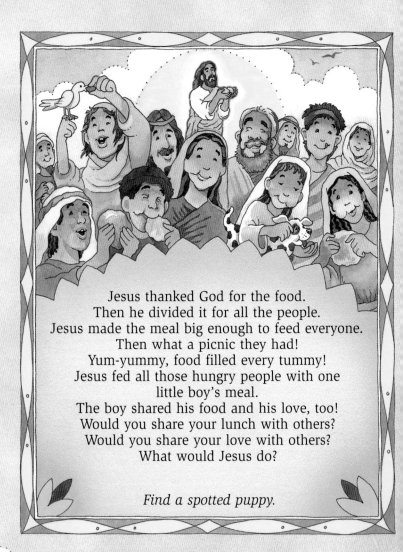

Jesus thanked God for the food.
Then he divided it for all the people.
Jesus made the meal big enough to feed everyone.
Then what a picnic they had!
Yum-yummy, food filled every tummy!
Jesus fed all those hungry people with one
little boy's meal.
The boy shared his food and his love, too!
Would you share your lunch with others?
Would you share your love with others?
What would Jesus do?

Find a spotted puppy.

Quiet Time

Night-Light has some questions.
- Who shared his food with Jesus?
- What did Jesus say?
  "Help other people freely."
- How can you help others?

Prayer Time

Dear God,
Please help us always share
and give to show we really care.
Amen.

Sleep Time

Tonight's Bible word is **give**.
Think about what you can give to others to show them God's love.
Sleep tight.

The Good Samaritan

Jesus said, "Show mercy." Luke 6:36

Jesus told a story about a man who was robbed.
Mean men stole the man's money and
left him lying hurt in the road.
Ouch! The poor hurt man! Who would help him?

Step, step, step. A village priest came along,
but he didn't stop—he just went on!
There's a hurt man lying there,
but who will stop to offer care?

Step, step, step. A Levite man came along,
but he didn't stop—he just went on!
There's a hurt man lying there,
but who will stop to offer care?

 Point to the hurt man.

Clip-clop, clippity-clop.
A Samaritan came
riding on a donkey.
Clip-clop, clippity-clop.
The Samaritan was the one to stop!
The good Samaritan gave the man water to drink
and covered his wounds.
Then the good Samaritan took the hurt man
to town and paid for his care.
What a nice man!
Jesus wants us to show we care
and help when someone
needs us there.

Quiet Time

Night-Light has some questions.

- Who helped the hurt man?
- What did Jesus say?
  "Show mercy."
- How can you show kindness
  and mercy to others?

Prayer Time

Dear God,
We're glad you're always there.
Help us show how much we care.
Amen.

Sleep Time

Tonight's Bible word is **mercy**.
Think about how happy Jesus is
when we're kind and show mercy
to others. Good night.

The Lost Sheep

Jesus said, "I will be with you always." Matthew 28:20

Jesus once told a story about a shepherd who had 100 sheep.
One day, the shepherd counted his sheep. "96, 97, 98, 99—
my, oh my! There's one I can't find!"
One of the sheep was lost!
The shepherd had many more sheep,
but he loved every one of them.
"I'll find my sheep—I'll look high and low.
But where should I start? I just don't know!"

The shepherd looked behind a stone,
he searched beside the brook.
The sad old shepherd searched the fields—
oh, where else should he look?
The shepherd looked up in a tree and behind a dandelion.
He searched and sought his little sheep—
he'd never stop his tryin'!

What animals do you see?

"Can you help me find my lamb?
I really love him so!
Do you see my little lamb?
If so, please let me know!"
There he is!
The shepherd was so happy to find his sheep,
that he whooped with joy—oh, boy!
He brought his sheep back to the flock,
then had a party to celebrate.
God is like that shepherd.
He wants us to stay close to him all the time.
Why? Because he loves us—every one!

Quiet Time

Night-Light has some questions.

- Why did the shepherd look for his lost sheep?
- What did Jesus say?
  "I will be with you always."
- Who wants you close to him?

Prayer Time

Dear God,
We want to be near you
and love you dearly
our whole lives through.
Amen.

Sleep Time

Tonight's Bible word is **near**. Think about how God wants to be near you and how good it feels to be close to God. Good night.

Jesus Loves Children

Jesus said, "Come to me." Matthew 19:14

Jesus was teaching the grown-ups about love.
All the mommies and daddies wanted their
little girls and boys to be close to Jesus.
But Jesus' friends said,
"Oh, no—make them go! Jesus is too busy!"

But Jesus said, "Come to me."
Jesus wanted the little children near.
Jesus hugged the children and loved them.
Jesus wanted the little children to learn about God.
So all the children came to Jesus.
Big kids, small kids, freckled-nosed tall kids.
Sad kids, happy kids, giggling-wiggling glad kids.
Kids with black hair, kids with brown;
kids from every tent and town.

 Which child has freckles?

Why did Jesus want the little
children to come to him?
Because Jesus loves little children.
Jesus loves each boy and girl—
every child around the world!
And Jesus knows children love him, too.
Thank you, Jesus—we do love you!

How many children do you see?

Quiet Time

Night-Light has some questions.
- Why did Jesus want little
  children to come to him?
- What did Jesus say?
  "Come to me."
- How do you tell Jesus you love him?

Prayer Time

Dear God,
Thank you for Jesus' love—
we love him so much, too.
Please help us find the ways to say,
"Jesus, we love you!"
Amen.

Sleep Time

Tonight's Bible word is **love**.
Think about how Jesus loves all
little children and how he
loves you, too!
Sleep tight.

Zaccheaus Is Forgiven

Jesus said, "Forgive other people." Luke 6:37

Once there was a grump named Zaccheaus.
"Hummmph! No one likes me!" said Zaccheaus.
The people didn't like Zaccheaus because
he took their money for taxes.
Zaccheaus heard that Jesus was coming to town.
Everyone was happy. But Zaccheaus didn't understand.
"Hummph! Why does everyone love Jesus?
Guess I'll take a peek!" he said.

So Zaccheaus climbed a tall tree!
He peeked through the branches.
When Jesus came to the tree, he said,
"Zaccheaus, come down. I'm going to your house."
Zaccheaus slid down the tree—zooop!
Everyone stared. Everyone was surprised!
Why would Jesus want to eat with grumpy Zaccheaus?

 Where is Zaccheaus?

Jesus ate with Zacchaeus because
Jesus loved Zacchaeus!
And Jesus forgave Zacchaeus for the
mean things he'd done.
Do you know what happened then?
Zacchaeus was so happy,
he gave back the people's money.
Yeah, Zacchaeus!

How many shiny coins do you see?

Quiet Time

Night-Light has some questions.
- Why did Jesus forgive
  Zacchaeus?
- What did Jesus say?
  "Forgive other people."
- Who can you forgive?

Prayer Time

Dear God,
Thank you for forgiving us
for all the times we disobey.
Help us to forgive others
in the same special way.
Amen.

Sleep Time

Tonight's Bible word is **forgive**.
Think about people you can forgive
and how happy it makes God.
Night-night!

Quiet Time

Night-Light has some questions.

- Who was coming to Jerusalem?
- What did Jesus say?
  "Be ready!"
- Who comes to live in our hearts?

Prayer Time

Dear God,
Thank you that Jesus is near
and that our hearts feel him here!
Help us be ready to tell him true—
"Jesus, we love you!"
Amen.

Sleep Time

Tonight's Bible word is **ready**.
Think about how you can always
be ready to love and follow Jesus.
Night-night.

Jesus Is Alive!

Jesus said, "I will be with you always." Matthew 28:20

Jesus' friends were sad.
It had been three days since Jesus died on the cross.
Several women who had followed
Jesus came to visit the tomb.
The women walked along sadly.
My, how they missed Jesus!
Then suddenly, something amazing happened!

At the tomb, the big stone had been rolled away.
And what do you think they saw?
An angel! A lightning-bright angel!
The angel said,
"Don't be afraid. I know you're looking for Jesus—
but he's not here. Jesus is alive!"
The women peeked inside the tomb.
What did they see?

 How many women do you see?

Nothing! The tomb was empty.
"Jesus is alive!" they shouted.
They were so happy that they ran to tell
Jesus' other friends the good news.
Jesus is alive today!
We're so happy, shout "Hooray!"
Jesus is alive today—
and forever!

How many friends do you see?

Quiet Time

Night-Light has some questions.
- What did the women see?
- What did Jesus say?
  "I will be with you always."
- Who is alive today and forever?

Prayer Time

Dear God,
We're so thankful we can say,
"Jesus is alive today!"
Amen.

Sleep Time

Tonight's Bible word is **alive**.
Think about how happy we are
that Jesus is alive.
Night-night.

Prayer Helps Peter

Jesus said, "Ask and you will receive." John 16:24

Peter was one of Jesus' friends.
He loved Jesus and wanted to tell others about him.
But a mean king didn't like Jesus and he didn't like Peter.
So the mean king tossed Peter in jail
and chained him to two rough, gruff guards.
Poor Peter. How could he ever get free?

Many people loved Jesus and they loved Peter, too.
When they heard that Peter was in jail,
what did they do?
They prayed and asked God to set Peter free.
Peter prayed, too—
then fell fast asleep between the two sleepy,
snoring guards.
Shhh, be very quiet—God is at work!
How would God help Peter escape?

 What happened to Peter?

God sent an angel to Peter.
The angel told Peter to wake up.
Then the chains fell off Peter's wrists.
Tiptoe, off we go—
did the mean guards awake?
Oh no, no, no!
God heard the prayers of the people
and helped Peter escape.
Then Peter was free to tell
more people about Jesus.
Yeah, Peter! Yeah, God!

Quiet Time

Night-Light has some questions.
- Why did God send the angel to help Peter?
- What did Jesus say?
  "Ask and you will receive."
- When do you pray?

Prayer Time

Dear God,
We're glad you're always there
to listen to our every prayer.
Amen.

Sleep Time

Tonight's Bible word is **prayer**.
Think about how God hears and
answers our prayers.
Night-night.

God bless you and good night!

Scripture Index